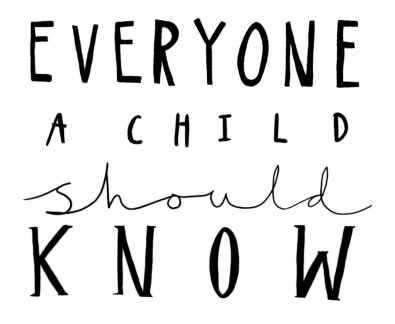
EVERYONE
A CHILD
should
KNOW

"A great little book... delightfully illustrated.
A must have book for every Christian home."
IAN FRY ~ ASSOCIATE MINISTER FOR FAMILIES, ST. EBBE'S CHURCH, OXFORD

"Here are 52 people I should know! Easy and fun to read with beautiful
pictures. It made me excited to be one of Jesus' friends too."
HELEN BUCKLEY ~ CHILDREN'S WORKER AND AUTHOR

"Ranging from the accomplished scientist and inventor George Washington
Carver to the famous Bible translator John Wycliffe, 'Everyone a Child Should
Know' introduces our youngest children to the men and women of history
whose lives exemplified I Corinthians 10:31, 'whatever you do, do it all for the
glory of God'. Clare Heath-Whyte has done a marvellous job retelling their
stories and the colourful illustrations of Jenny Brake are simply delightful."
MARTY MACHOWSKI ~ PASTOR AND AUTHOR OF SEVERAL BOOKS INCLUDING "THE OLOGY"

"Reading this book surrounded me with a wonderful 'cloud of witnesses': Christians whose stories inspired and encouraged me. Like me, you'll want to know more about them and how to live every day for our friend Jesus."

LIZ COX ~ CHAIR OF THE MIDLANDS WOMEN'S CONVENTIONS

"Reading 'Everyone a child should know' with your children will be a brilliant way to ignite an interest in some heroes of the Christian faith and may well inspire them to live a life that pleases Jesus, with whatever gifts he has given them and in whatever circumstances he places them."

TAMAR POLLARD ~ CHILDREN'S WORKER, CHRIST CHURCH FULWOOD, SHEFFIELD

A varied Christian reading habit is healthy for adults. This book adds basic Christian biographies to what we can read to our young children. What a great addition to Bible stories and systematic theology.

TIM CHAPMAN ~ VICAR, CHRIST CHURCH SOUTH CAMBS

Illustrations copyright © 2017 by Jenny Brake
Text copyright © 2017 by Clare Heath-Whyte

First published in Great Britain in 2017

British Library Cataloguing in Publication Data
A record for this book is available from the British Library

ISBN: 978-1-911272-60-1
Designed by Diane Warnes
Printed in China

10Publishing, a division of 10ofthose.com
Unit C, Tomlinson Road, Leyland, PR25 2DY, England
Email: info@10ofthose.com
Website: www.10ofthose.com

EVERYONE
A CHILD
should
KNOW

WRITTEN BY CLARE HEATH-WHYTE
ILLUSTRATED BY JENNY BRAKE

10 Publishing
a division of **10** of those.com

Contents

A note to parents and carers

There are loads of Christian biographies around for older children and adults, but almost none for younger children - yet it is never too early to introduce the next generation to some of the heroes of the faith. Here we meet fifty-two Christian men and women (one to read every week of the year ...) from all walks of life, who wanted to live for their "friend Jesus". There are missionaries and martyrs (although fewer martyrs than you might find in a book for older children!), writers, reformers, politicians, preachers and poets. There are sporty people, arty people, brilliant people and very ordinary people. There are people from hundreds of years ago and people still living today. Some are very well known while some are almost unheard of. Jesus has always had, and always will have, friends in all shapes, sizes and colours, from all different countries and backgrounds. My hope and prayer is that, as you read about these remarkable men and women with your child, you will both realise that anyone who is "Jesus' friend" can do remarkable things for him - even you!

"Jesus Christ is the same yesterday and today and forever."
Hebrews 13:8

"The LORD is my light and my salvation - whom shall I fear?
The LORD is the stronghold of my life - of whom shall I be afraid?"
Psalm 27:1

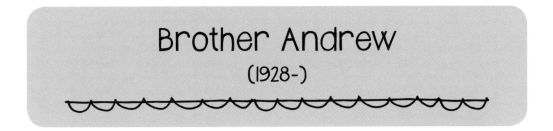

Brother Andrew
(1928-)

What do you like most about going to church? Bible stories? Singing? Meeting friends?

Did you know there are some countries in the world where Jesus' friends aren't allowed to meet together, or read the Bible, or tell other people about Jesus? When Brother Andrew found out how hard it was for people in those places to be Jesus' friends he wanted to help. Jesus' friends needed Bibles to read - but how could he get Bibles into those countries? He knew it would be difficult and he knew it would be dangerous - but he knew that his friend Jesus would look after him.

Time after time Andrew took cars stuffed with Bibles into countries where Bibles were not allowed. There were soldiers and spies and secret police; it was difficult; it was dangerous. Time after time Andrew's friend Jesus looked after him - and the Bibles! Time after time soldiers and spies and secret police didn't notice all the Bibles stuffed into the cars. Time after time carloads of Bibles reached Jesus' friends.

In some of those countries it is now safe to be Jesus' friends - but there are still lots where it is not safe at all. It is still difficult and dangerous to help Jesus' friends in those countries, but Brother Andrew and his friends are still helping - and their friend Jesus is still looking after them!

"Do not remember the sins of my youth and my rebellious ways;
according to your love remember me, for you, LORD, are good."

Psalm 25:7

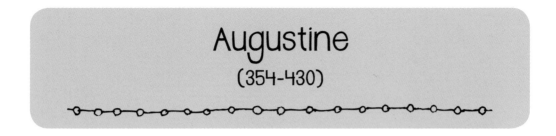

Augustine
(354-430)

Do you ever get told off by your teacher or by your mum? Do you sometimes not do what you are told? Some children find it easy to be good - some don't!

Augustine didn't find it easy to be good. He enjoyed doing naughty things. His mother was Jesus' friend - but Augustine wasn't. He was having too much fun to bother with Jesus. He took things that weren't his. He didn't do what his mother told him. He thought this was funny. It made his mother sad. She asked Jesus to show Augustine that the things he did were wrong.

Augustine grew up. He still did naughty things. He still made his mother sad. She still asked Jesus to help. Sometimes Augustine felt bad - being naughty wasn't always fun - but he didn't want to stop just yet ...

Then, one day, he was in the garden. He heard a child say, "Pick it up and read it!" But there was no one there. What could it mean? Then he saw his friend's Bible on the ground. He picked it up and read it! He read that Jesus could forgive him for all the bad things he had done. He read that Jesus could help him stop doing bad things. He became Jesus' friend. His mother was so happy.

Even though he had been a naughty boy, Augustine became one of the world's most famous Bible teachers! Jesus can change anybody.

"For the LORD takes delight in his people;
he crowns the humble with victory."

Psalm 149:4

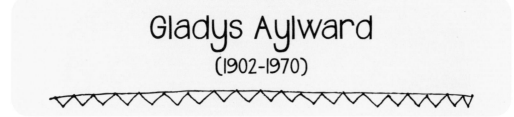

Gladys Aylward
(1902-1970)

Are you good at lots of things, or a few things, or do you feel just ordinary?

Gladys Aylward was just ordinary. She was not very clever - just ordinary. She was not very rich - just ordinary. Her job wasn't special - just ordinary. She worked as a maid in a rich home, tidying and cleaning. But Gladys had an extraordinary friend - Jesus - and she wanted to go to China to tell people there all about him. But no one wanted her to go to China with them - they thought she was too ordinary - so Gladys went on her own.

With the help of her extraordinary friend Jesus, ordinary Gladys did some extraordinary things. She ran a hotel in the middle of nowhere and told Bible stories to the travellers. She worked for the government inspecting feet! While she checked their feet she told the people all about her friend Jesus. She stopped prisoners fighting in a prison. She looked after more than a hundred children who had no one else to love them. When war came to China she kept her children safe from danger by walking with them for days and days and days across the mountains to escape the fighting. Gladys had some extraordinary adventures!

Some people thought Gladys was too ordinary - but Jesus didn't. Jesus can help his ordinary friends like you, me and Gladys to do extraordinary things for him.

"Praise him with the sounding of the trumpet,
praise him with the harp and lyre ..."
Psalm 150:3

Johann Sebastian Bach
(1685-1750)

Can you play a musical instrument? Do you have lessons on the piano or recorder? Perhaps you just like making music for fun.

When Johann Sebastian Bach was growing up in Germany he loved playing music. He played the violin ... and the viola ... and the organ ... and the harpsichord ... and the clavichord (which was like an old-fashioned piano) ... and he was really good at singing! Johann Sebastian loved music, but he loved Jesus too. He wanted to use his music to show how much he loved his friend Jesus.

When he grew up, Johann Sebastian's job was to play music and sing in church. He didn't just play and sing, he wrote new music too. He wrote music to go with the bits of the Bible that were read each Sunday. He wrote new music for old church songs. He wrote special happy music for Easter Sunday and Christmas. He wrote special sad music for Good Friday when Jesus died. He wrote all his music to show people how much his friend Jesus loved them too. Sometimes Johann Sebastian's music didn't have Bible words and wasn't played in church. He still wanted his music to show how much he loved Jesus. He knew that Jesus helped him write all his beautiful music.

Why not ask Jesus to help you make up a tune to show him how much you love him too?

"A father to the fatherless, a defender of widows,
is God in his holy dwelling. God sets the lonely in families ..."
Psalm 68:5-6

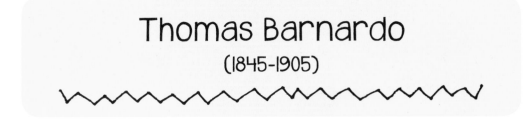
What is your bedroom like? Do you have a room of your own or do you share it? Is your bed comfy? What else is in your room?

There are some children who don't have a bedroom at all. They don't have a bed to sleep on - or even a house to live in. In London, when Thomas Barnardo was alive, there were lots and lots of children with nowhere to live and no one to look after them.

Thomas wanted to go to China to help people there - until he saw how much the children in London needed his help. He knew that his friend Jesus loved children very much - so Thomas loved children too. Thomas knew that Jesus never turned anyone away - so Thomas never turned anyone away. He always found room if a child needed help. He always found room for children who had no home. He always found room for children who were poor, sad, sick or alone. In the end he set up more than a hundred homes for boys and girls who had nowhere to live. He even made a special village to care for fifteen hundred girls!

Thousands and thousands of children now had somewhere to live and someone to love them. Thousands and thousands of children were taught to read and write - and taught all about Thomas' friend Jesus.

"You are my hiding-place; you will protect me from trouble and surround me with songs of deliverance."

Psalm 32:7

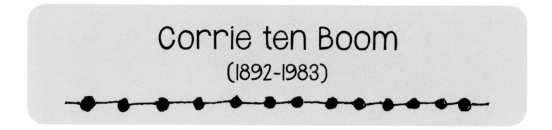

Corrie ten Boom
(1892-1983)

Do you like hiding? Do you have a favourite hiding place? Behind the sofa? Under the bed? In the wardrobe?

Corrie ten Boom had a very special hiding place - a tiny little space in her bedroom. It was hidden and secret. Corrie's hiding place wasn't for playing games - it was for keeping people safe. Corrie's family lived in Holland. Bad people took over the country and did bad things. They wanted to kill all Jewish people (who come from the family of Abraham in the Old Testament). Corrie's family were Jesus' friends and knew Jesus thought this was very wrong. They looked after as many Jewish people as they could. They fed them, they hid them and they helped them escape.

One day soldiers came. They sent the whole family to prison for helping the Jews - but the Jewish people were safe in Corrie's special hiding place. Corrie and her sister Betsie weren't safe. In prison they were cold; they were hungry; they were ill; they were treated very badly. Betsie told Corrie that their friend Jesus was with them - even when they were cold, hungry, ill and badly treated. Betsie told Corrie that Jesus wanted her to love, not hate.

Betsie died in prison. But when Corrie was set free she spent her whole life telling her story; telling how Jesus was with her when she was cold, ill and hungry; telling how we should always love and not hate - just like her friend Jesus.

"The poor will see and be glad - you who seek God,
may your hearts live!"

Psalm 69:32

William and Catherine Booth
(1829-1912 and 1829-1890)

I wonder what your friends are like. Are they just like you - or are they all quite different?

William and Catherine Booth knew that when their friend Jesus was on earth he had lots of friends. Often they were not the kind of friends you would expect - sad people; poor people; lonely people; even bad people. But William and Catherine didn't see many people like that in churches in England. People like that hadn't heard that they could be Jesus' friends too. They hadn't heard that Jesus could forgive them, love them and help them to change. So William and Catherine decided to tell them!

They told the saddest, the poorest, the loneliest and the baddest (!) people that they could be Jesus' friends too. Some people didn't want to listen - they shouted and yelled and threw things. It was so dangerous that William said it was like being in an army - they became known as the Salvation Army. But they kept going even when it was dangerous and hard. They showed these people that Jesus loved them by giving them food, by giving them clothes and by giving them work. People listened. Soon Jesus had thousands and thousands of new, very different friends.

The Salvation Army spread all over the world and is still helping all kinds of different people to see that they can be Jesus' friends too.

"My heart is stirred by a noble theme as I recite my verses for the king; my tongue is the pen of a skilful writer."

Psalm 45:1

Anne Bradstreet
(1612-1672)

Have you ever written a poem? What was it about? Did it rhyme?

Anne Bradstreet wrote loads of poems all about the things she loved - her husband, her children and her friend Jesus. Anne was the first person in America ever to have poems published in a book!

Anne didn't always live in America. She was born in a castle in England. She had a beautiful home, beautiful clothes and lots of beautiful books. She travelled to America with her family and her new husband when she was eighteen. The long journey was dangerous, her new home was cold and her new clothes were dull, but Anne knew her friend Jesus was still with her. She had to move house again and again, but Anne knew her friend Jesus was still with her. She was ill again and again, but Anne knew her friend Jesus was still with her. Her husband had to go far away to work again and again, but Anne knew her friend Jesus was still with her - and with her eight children! Even when her house burnt to the ground Anne knew her friend Jesus was still with her!

All this time Anne was writing poems. They were about how she loved her husband, how she loved her children and how she loved and trusted her friend Jesus - even when her house burnt down!

"Even though I walk through the darkest valley, I will fear no evil, for you are with me; your rod and your staff, they comfort me."
Psalm 23:4

Have you ever been on a long journey? Where did you go? Was it exciting - or was it a bit boring?

John Bunyan wrote a book about a journey. It wasn't about a journey to visit his grandma or go on holiday. His book was about a dangerous and difficult journey to be with Jesus in heaven. It's called "A Pilgrim's Progress". It is one of the most famous books in the world!

John knew that being Jesus' friend could be difficult and could be dangerous. In those days, in England, you could only tell people about Jesus if you had a special piece of paper. John didn't have a special piece of paper. He told people about Jesus anyway. He was put in prison for years and years and years.

During those years and years and years in prison he wrote his famous book - the story of a man called Pilgrim and his journey to be with Jesus in heaven. Pilgrim's journey is difficult - but he keeps going. Pilgrim's journey is dangerous - but he keeps going. He keeps going until he is safe and sound with his friend Jesus in heaven. Knowing he would be with his friend Jesus in heaven kept John Bunyan going when things were dangerous and difficult - even when he was in prison. John knew Jesus would get him to heaven safe and sound. Do you?

"Open my eyes that I may see
wonderful things in your law."
Psalm 119:18

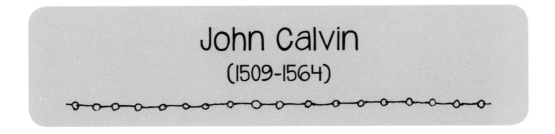

John Calvin
(1509-1564)

Do you like working hard at school? Do you think reading, writing and sums are fun? Jesus can really use friends like you!

John Calvin liked working hard. He liked reading very clever books; he liked thinking very clever thoughts; he liked writing very clever things down. Then he became Jesus' friend. He loved reading the Bible; he loved thinking about the Bible; he loved writing about the Bible.

In his country, France, in those days, that was a very dangerous thing to do. People didn't like the Bible or care what it said. John had to run away. Where would he go? He was asked to teach the Bible in Geneva, in Switzerland - a town a long way from home - but most people there weren't Jesus' friends and didn't want to do what the Bible said - yet. He had to run away again. He kept reading the Bible; he kept thinking about the Bible; he kept writing about the Bible. He became quite famous. Now Geneva wanted him back! Now Geneva wanted John to teach them the Bible.

He worked very hard - speaking and teaching and writing about the Bible. Little by little people became Jesus' friends. Little by little people wanted to do what the Bible said. Geneva became full of Jesus' friends living Jesus' way - all because clever John Calvin worked hard for Jesus.

"The earth is the LORD's, and everything in it,
the world, and all who live in it."

Psalm 24:1

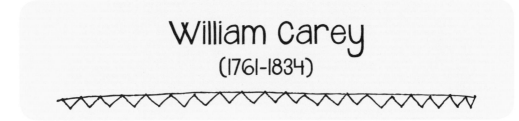

William Carey
(1761-1834)

Have you ever been to a different country on holiday? Which country was it? How did you get there?

Nowadays it's easy to visit different countries. When William Carey was alive it was not easy at all - there were no buses or trains, cars or planes. Most people only travelled a few miles in their whole lives. William was a shoemaker; he lived in a little English town; he had a wife and children; he had never travelled anywhere. But William knew that people the other side of the world needed to know about his friend Jesus - and no one else seemed to care. So William the shoemaker left his little town with his wife and children and travelled to India, on the other side of the world.

To tell people in India about his friend Jesus he needed to learn their languages - so he did. He needed to put the Bible in words they understood - so he did. He needed to print new Bibles - so he did. He did whatever he could to show the people in India that they could be Jesus' friends too. It was hard; it was hard for him; it was hard for his wife and children - but he did it.

Little by little other people went to other countries to tell them about Jesus too - all because shoemaker William did it first!

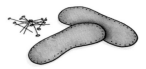

"He raises the poor from the dust and
lifts the needy from the ash heap ..."
Psalm 113:7

Have you ever felt embarrassed? Was it something you did or said? Did your face go pink?

One day Amy Carmichael felt embarrassed. She helped a poor, shabby, dirty woman. That was a good and kind thing to do, but Amy was embarrassed because her friends saw her with such a poor, shabby, dirty person. Then Amy remembered her friend Jesus and how he loved poor, shabby and dirty people as much as he loved her. So Amy decided to help poor, shabby and dirty people, and tell them all about her friend Jesus.

First Amy helped poor people near her home in Belfast in Northern Ireland. Then she helped poor people in Manchester in England. Then she decided to help poor people in other countries and tell them about her friend Jesus. She travelled to Japan and then to India.

In India Amy cared for the poorest of the poor and the shabbiest of the shabby - little girls whose parents were so poor they gave their daughters to Hindu temples. These little girls were treated very badly and had to do some very bad things. Amy rescued them, cared for them and told them all about Jesus.

When Amy became too ill to work, she wrote books and songs and poems to help even more people trust her friend Jesus.

"He makes grass grow for the cattle, and plants for people to cultivate - bringing forth food from the earth ..."

Psalm 104:14

George Washington Carver
(About 1861-1943)

What do you like spreading on your toast, or eating in sandwiches? Jam? Marmalade? Maybe peanut butter?

George Washington Carver became very famous by teaching people how to grow peanuts and make things out of peanuts - like peanut butter, and paint and plastic!

George was a famous scientist and inventor, but when he was born he was a slave - he belonged to someone else. The family that owned him was white - he was black. In America, where he lived, all slaves were set free when he was a little boy - but because he was black there were still lots of things he couldn't do. But he could be Jesus' friend.

Jesus had made George good at reading and writing and thinking - but he couldn't go to the local school. So George walked and walked and walked until he found a school he could go to. He learnt and learnt and learnt at different schools and colleges until it was time to choose a job. What should he do? He was good at playing music, painting pictures as well as science and inventing. How could he choose? He chose to help people like his friend Jesus did. He chose to help poor farmers grow peanuts and make things out of peanuts so they could have enough money and enough food for their families.
I wonder what job you will choose.

"Lead me, LORD, in your righteousness because of my
enemies - make straight your way before me."
Psalm 5:8

John Chrysostom
(349-407)

Do you have a nickname? Maybe it's just a silly name; maybe it's a shorter name; maybe it says something about what you are like?

John Chrysostom was not John's real name. Chrysostom was a nickname. It means "golden mouth" in his language. John was given that name because he was so good at telling people about Jesus - golden words came out of his mouth! People loved listening to him. They listened at Christmas when John told them about Jesus being born. They listened at Easter when John told them how Jesus died and rose again. They even listened when John told them they were not living the way Jesus wanted!

John became so famous that he was asked to be the leader of the biggest church in Constantinople, the biggest town around. The people there liked John telling them about Jesus being born at Christmas and Jesus dying and rising again at Easter; but they did not like being told they were not living the way Jesus wanted! The powerful leaders didn't want to hear that they should look after poor people and be kind and generous. John told them anyway!

So the powerful leaders sent John away. John wrote letters to remind them how Jesus wanted them to live. They sent him further away! But John never stopped teaching about Jesus - even when it was hard.

"I will sing the LORD'S praise,
for he has been good to me."
Psalm 13:6

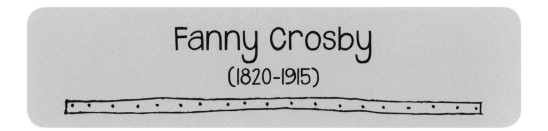

Fanny Crosby
(1820-1915)

Do you like singing in church or assembly at school? Singing is brilliant! Songs can help us learn about Jesus and help us to tell him how great he is. Do you have a favourite song about Jesus?

Fanny Crosby didn't just like singing songs about Jesus - she liked writing them too! She wrote thousands and thousands of songs which were sung by millions and millions of people - and still are today! But Fanny couldn't write her songs down because Fanny couldn't see. Her eyes hadn't worked since she was a baby. Fanny couldn't see, but that didn't stop her doing things for her friend Jesus. She made up poems and songs in her head and someone else wrote them down.

Her songs were all about Jesus: how he died for us; how much he loves us; how kind he is; how he forgives us; how great he is. Fanny wanted people to sing her songs so they could find out how to become Jesus' friends too.

Fanny became very, very famous - but she didn't want to be rich or live in a big house. When Fanny was old she lived in a very small house where the very poorest people lived so that she could show the people there that Jesus loved them too.

Why don't you try to write a song about Jesus like Fanny did?

"My comfort in my suffering is this:
Your promise preserves my life."

Psalm 119:50

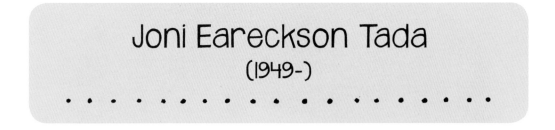

Joni Eareckson Tada
(1949-)

Do you like running and jumping? Do you like swimming and kicking a ball about?

Joni Eareckson Tada liked all those things too. She liked to run and swim and ride horses and play tennis. But then, one day, she dived into a lake and hurt her neck. She hurt her neck so badly that she couldn't move her legs or her feet. She couldn't move her arms or her hands either. That made Joni very sad - then she remembered her friend Jesus.

She knew that Jesus was with her and loved her. She knew that bad things happened to Jesus too and that he understood. She knew that one day, when she went to live with her friend Jesus forever, she would be able to run and jump again.

So Joni has spent her life telling people about her friend Jesus. In books, on the radio, in talks and through pictures painted with a brush in her mouth, Joni has told people how Jesus is always with her, always loves her and always helps her. She has told them how Jesus loves everybody - whether they can run or not; whether they can jump or not; whether they can see or not; whether they can hear or not - and how one day Jesus' friends will all run and jump and hear and see when they live with him forever.

"For the king trusts in the LORD; through the unfailing love of the Most High he will not be shaken."

Psalm 21:7

Edward VI
(1537-1553)

What would you do if you were a king or a queen? Live in a castle? Wear lovely clothes? Tell people what to do?

Edward VI was a real king. His father was one of the most famous English kings - Henry VIII. Henry died when Edward was only nine, so Edward then became king. Edward did live in a castle, he did wear lovely clothes and he did tell people what to do, but the most important thing Edward did was to help people in England find out about his friend Jesus.

Edward was only a boy, and he was only king for six years because he died when he was just fifteen - but he did everything he could to help people find out about Jesus. Edward was very clever and knew all about the Bible. He made sure that English Bibles were in every church so that ordinary people could find out about Jesus. He made sure church services helped people understand how they could be Jesus' friends and helped them understand the Bible. He gave important jobs to Jesus' friends who would help him rule England in the way Jesus wanted.

Edward was only a boy, he was only king for six years and he died when he was just fifteen - but while he was king more and more people in England became Jesus' friends.

"Precious in the sight of the LORD is
the death of his faithful servants."

Psalm 116:15

Jim and Elisabeth Elliott
(1927-1956 and 1926-2015)

Do you have something that is very special to you? A toy? A teddy? A friend? Your family?

Jim Elliott thought his friends were very special. He thought his wife Elisabeth and baby Valerie were very special. I'm sure when he was little he thought his toys and teddies were special too. But Jim knew that his friend Jesus was the most special of all.

Jim wanted to tell people who lived in the middle of a South American jungle that they could be Jesus' friends. Jim and his friends flew an aeroplane over the jungle. They dropped presents to the people who lived there. They learnt their language and shouted out, "Hello" from the plane. After months and months of doing this they landed there. They met some of the people and they were ready to tell them about Jesus. But then ... a very terrible thing happened - the people from the jungle killed Jim and his friends.

Jim's wife, Elisabeth, didn't hate the people from the jungle. She loved them, because her friend Jesus loved them. Elisabeth, with little Valerie, went into the jungle to tell the people who killed Jim that Jesus wanted to be their friend. She cared for them, worked with them and told them about Jesus. They listened, and some of them became Jesus' friends too.

"I will speak of your statutes before kings
and will not be put to shame ..."

Psalm 119:46

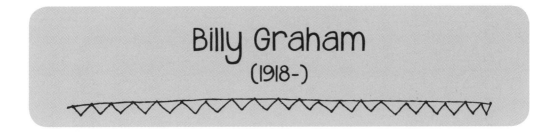

Billy Graham
(1918-)

Have you ever met anyone famous? Who was it? If you haven't, what famous person would you most like to meet?

During his time as a travelling Bible teacher, Billy Graham met loads and loads of famous people. In fact he met some of the most important people in the world - the queen of England; the leaders of China, Russia, India, Germany, North Korea and Japan; and lots and lots of American presidents. What did Billy talk about with all these famous people? His friend Jesus, of course!

Billy became as famous as all the important people he met, but when he was little he lived with his ordinary family, on an ordinary farm and wasn't famous at all. Billy became famous because he was so good at telling people about his friend Jesus. He didn't just tell famous people. Billy told billions of ordinary people about his friend Jesus too - on the radio; in films; in books; on television; in small meetings; in big meetings; and in humungous meetings with thousands and thousands of people. Billy told people at home in America - and in Asia, Europe, Australia and any other place you can think of!

Everywhere he went Billy said the same thing - that Jesus loves us so much that he died so that we can be his friends forever. Billions of people heard that message and millions of them became Jesus' friends.

"Though an army besiege me, my heart will not fear;
though war break out against me, even then I will be confident."

Psalm 27:3

Argula von Grumbach
(1492-about 1557)

Have you ever been left out - of a game, or a chat, or a party? It can be hard, can't it?

Argula von Grumbach was left out. People didn't want to be her friend - even her family was mean to her. Argula had found out how to be Jesus' friend by reading the Bible. But where she lived in Germany you could be put in prison - or worse - for even reading the Bible for yourself, so not many people did!

One day, a young man who was Jesus' friend was put in prison for reading the Bible. Argula wanted to help him - but what could she do? She asked some men who were Jesus' friends to help. They didn't. What could she do now? She wrote letters - very long letters - to very important people. In her letters she wrote that it was good to be Jesus' friend. In her letters she wrote that it was good to read the Bible. Thousands and thousands of people read her letters. She became very famous. But important people, and even her family, tried to stop her writing her letters. They said horrid things about her. They said they would hurt her. And they wouldn't change their minds and let people read the Bible.

Argula was left out - but she knew her friend Jesus was with her. Argula was left out - but she still stood up for Jesus and his friends. Will you?

God's words "are more precious than gold, than much pure gold;
they are sweeter than honey, than honey from the honeycomb."
Psalm 19:10

Have you got a favourite book? Why is it so special? Is it the pictures, or the story, or because someone special gave it to you?

Mary Jones had a favourite book. Her favourite book was the Bible. She knew the Bible could teach her all about God. But Mary couldn't read it herself. There was no school in her village to teach her. So Mary prayed ... and prayed ... and prayed. A school was built. Mary learnt to read. But Mary didn't have a Bible. Her family was too poor to buy one. So Mary worked ... and worked ... and worked ... to get money to buy her own Bible. But there was nowhere in her village to buy a Bible. So Mary had to go to a town where she could buy one. In those days there were no cars or trains or bikes, and she was too poor to have a horse. Mary had to walk ... and walk ... and walk. She walked all the way over the mountains to find the man who could sell her a Bible. Her feet hurt, she was very tired, she had no money left, but at last she had her very own Bible to read. She was so happy!

Mary really knew that the Bible is the best book ever!

"All the ends of the earth will remember and turn to the LORD,
and all the families of the nations will bow down before him ..."

Psalm 22:27

Adoniram Judson
(1788-1850)

Who first told you about Jesus? Your parents? Your friend? Someone at church or school?

Adoniram Judson didn't become Jesus' friend until he was a grown-up, but he had always known about Jesus - from his parents, from church and from school. But Adoniram knew that some people in the world would never hear about Jesus from their parents, from church or from school. He knew that there were places in the world where almost nobody had heard about Jesus at all - places like Burma. No one from America had ever gone overseas to tell people about Jesus before - but Adoniram decided to go.

Burma was very different from America. The people spoke a different language - so Adoniram learnt it. The people wore different clothes - so Adoniram wore them. No one knew about Jesus - so Adoniram told them. He told lots and lots of Burmese people - but nobody wanted to be Jesus' friend. He told more and more Burmese people. Finally, after six whole years of telling Burmese people about Jesus, one Burmese man became Jesus' friend.

Adoniram kept going. He put the Bible into the Burmese language so more people could find out about Jesus. He was ill, he was put in prison, his wife died, his children died - but Adoniram kept going. By the time Adoniram died thousands of Burmese people had become Jesus' friends.

"LORD my God, I take refuge in you; save
and deliver me from all who pursue me ..."

Psalm 7:1

Do you like adventure stories? Stories that are exciting and a bit scary?

John Knox's life was like an adventure story in a book. John Knox's life was exciting and sometimes very scary indeed! John was Jesus' friend and trusted God's word the Bible - and in Scotland, when John was alive, that was a very dangerous thing to do because the leaders didn't want people to trust the Bible but to do what they said instead.

John could be quite fierce and John could be quite stubborn - and John never gave up. John never gave up trusting his friend Jesus and teaching God's word the Bible. John was taken prisoner and was a slave on a French ship; he trusted Jesus and taught the Bible. John was asked to preach to the king of England; he trusted Jesus and taught the Bible. He had to escape to another country; he trusted Jesus and taught the Bible. Back in Scotland he knew he could be put in prison at any time; he trusted Jesus and taught the Bible. More and more people in Scotland became Jesus' friends and wanted to hear John's talks; he still trusted Jesus and taught the Bible.

Finally, because John and his friends would not give up, Scotland became a country where it was safe to be Jesus' friend and trust the Bible.

"The fool says in his heart,
'There is no God.'"

Psalm 14:1

Do you ever make up stories? What are they about? Princes and princesses? Knights and dragons? Robots and dinosaurs?

Clive Staples Lewis always made up stories - even when he was a little boy. He even made up a new name for himself - Jack! Some stories were about talking animals; some were about heroes; some were about magic and mystery. As he grew up he thought that Jesus was just another story. He didn't know that Jesus was real and that he could be his friend.

Jack was very clever. When he was a grown-up he was a teacher in a university (where people go to learn more after they are too old for school). The other teachers were clever too - and some were Jesus' friends. Jack wondered whether maybe Jesus was real after all ... Soon Jack became Jesus' friend too.

Now Jack wanted everyone to know that Jesus was real. He wrote books; he gave talks; he spoke on the radio. People read his books, listened to his talks and heard him on the radio - and became Jesus' friends. Jack wanted boys and girls to be Jesus' friends too, so he made up stories - stories with talking animals, heroes, magic and mystery in a place called Narnia - but the stories were really all about Jesus. Maybe one day you could read Jack's stories about Narnia for yourself.

"I run in the path of your commands,
for you have broadened my understanding."

Psalm 119:32

Eric Liddell
(1902-1945)

Are you a fast runner? God makes some people who can run fast and some people who can't. Sometimes, like on sports day at school, it can seem that running fast is the most important thing in the world. It isn't really - it is much more important to be Jesus' friend and live for him.

Eric Liddell was a very, very fast runner. He was the fastest runner in the world and won a gold medal at the Olympic Games. He loved running, but he loved his friend Jesus even more! Because Eric was a good runner people wanted to listen to what he said. Eric told them about Jesus.

Eric was a famous man, but he went to China - a country a long way away - where nobody had even heard of him. He wanted to tell the people there about Jesus too. It was a very dangerous place to be. There was fighting and Eric was put in prison. It was horrid, but Eric now had more people to tell about Jesus. Eric was cold and hungry and soon he became very ill, but he always knew that Jesus was looking after him.

When Eric died people said how great he was because he could run fast. Eric knew that it was much greater to be Jesus' friend and tell people all about him.

"Your wife will be like a fruitful vine within your house;
your children will be like olive shoots round your table."

Psalm 128:3

Katie Luther
(1499-1552)

All mums are really special, aren't they? What's special about your mum? Her cooking? Her caring? Her cuddles?

Katie Luther never knew her mum - she died when Katie was a little girl. Katie thought she would never be a mum either. Katie was a nun. A nun is someone who has said she will never marry or have children and who lives in a big house with other nuns. When Katie lived, people thought you could only be Jesus' special friend if you didn't get married or have children.

Then Katie found out from the Bible that she could be Jesus' special friend whether she was a nun or not, whether she was married or not, and whether she had children or not. So Katie got married - to Martin Luther. He was a very busy and important man. She looked after him when he was well, when he was ill, when he was happy and when he was grumpy. They had six children. She looked after them when they were well, ill, happy and grumpy. Lots of people lived with them, stayed with them and visited them. She looked after all of them too. She cooked, cleaned and cared for them all. She even ran her own farm and made her own beer!

Katie showed her family and friends that she loved her friend Jesus by loving them too.

"When we were overwhelmed by sins,
you forgave us our transgressions."

Psalm 65:3

Martin Luther
(1483-1546)

It's great being Jesus' friend isn't it? It's great to know that he loves you and forgives you even when you haven't been a very good friend to him.

Martin Luther wanted to be Jesus' friend - but he didn't know how. The people in charge of the church in Luther's country, Germany - and in all the other countries - had got it wrong and said that to be Jesus' friend you had to do everything they said and never do bad things. Martin tried and tried but he still did bad things - we all do!

Then Martin looked in his Bible. In those days the Bible was written in an old language, but Martin was clever and he could read it. He read that Jesus died to take away the bad things that he did. He read that he could be Jesus' friend if he asked Jesus to forgive him for those bad things. He was so happy.

Martin told the people in charge of the church that they were wrong. That made them very cross. They tried to stop Martin. But Martin wanted everybody to know how they could be Jesus' friends too. He didn't stop. He was very brave. He put the Bible in his language. He wrote books and songs and letters. Soon whole countries had churches where they could find out how to be Jesus' friends. Thank you, God, for Martin Luther!

"I proclaim your saving acts in the great assembly;
I do not seal my lips, LORD, as you know."

Psalm 40:9

Dwight L. Moody
(1837-1899)

What is the highest number you can count to? Ten? A hundred? A thousand? A million?

When Dwight Moody was around you would have had to count up to very big numbers indeed. Dwight told a hundred million people about Jesus and a million of them became Jesus' friends!

Dwight became Jesus' friend when he was a young man working in a shoe shop. Straight away he started telling his friends and family how they could be Jesus' friends too. Soon he set up a Sunday school for the poor children in Chicago in America, where he lived. Lots and lots of children heard how they could be Jesus' friend too. He set up a meeting for grown-ups, and lots and lots of them heard how they could be Jesus' friend. He travelled to England, Scotland and Ireland, and lots and lots and lots of people came to hear him tell them how they could be Jesus' friends too. When he went back to America even more people came to hear him - lots and lots and lots and lots, thousands and thousands and thousands, millions and millions and millions!

Dwight set up a college to train other people to tell even more millions and millions how Jesus could be their friend too. Who could you tell about Jesus today?

"The fear of the LORD is the beginning of wisdom; all who follow his precepts have good understanding. To him belongs eternal praise."

Psalm 111:10

Hannah More

(1745-1833)

Have you ever been in a play or a show? What did you do? Was it fun?

When Hannah More was young she wrote lots of plays. Famous people in London liked her plays, so Hannah became famous too. Everyone thought Hannah was very clever, very funny and very wise.

Then Hannah met people who were Jesus' friends - people like William Wilberforce and John Newton, who you can find out about in this book. Hannah became Jesus' friend too. She still wrote plays - but now she didn't write plays so that people thought she was clever, or to make her famous. Now she also wrote little books to help people find out about Jesus and how to live for him - and, because she was famous for being clever, people read them. Now she also wrote poems about how wrong it was to buy and sell people as slaves - and, because she was famous for being clever, people read them.

But Hannah knew that a lot of people couldn't read at all. They couldn't read her books. They couldn't read the Bible. So Hannah started schools to teach them - and, because she was famous for being clever, other people copied her and set up schools too.

Hannah was famous and she was clever - but she knew it was far more important to be Jesus' friend.

"He provides food for those who fear him;
he remembers his covenant for ever."

Psalm 111:5

George Müller
(1805-1898)

If you are hungry who do you ask for a snack? Your mum? Your dad? Someone else who looks after you?

George Müller knew that the best person to ask when he needed anything was his friend Jesus. George was born in Germany, but came to England to tell people about his friend Jesus. He wasn't paid and never asked anyone for money. He asked Jesus to give him what he needed - and Jesus did!

George set up schools for boys and girls, so they could learn to read and write and find out about his friend Jesus. He asked Jesus to give him the money that he needed - and Jesus did! George set up homes for boys and girls with no families. He asked Jesus to give him the money that he needed - and Jesus did! One day George prayed for food for the children. The doorbell rang - it was the baker wanting to give them bread. It rang again - it was the milkman wanting to give them milk! George looked after thousands of children. They always had food; they always had clothes; they even had enough money to give away to people who needed it more!

George asked Jesus to help him with food, money and clothes - even the drains and holes in the roof too - and he did! George knew that Jesus always looks after his friends.

"Mightier than the thunder of the great waters, mightier than the breakers of the sea - the LORD on high is mighty."

Psalm 93:4

John Newton
(1725-1807)

Have you ever been on a boat? Have you ever been on a boat when there have been big waves and lots of wind and rain? It can be quite scary.

John Newton was a sailor. He was used to being on boats - even with big waves. His boats carried people from Africa to America, but not for holidays. The people on his boats were sold for money so they belonged to other people. That was a very bad thing to do! John Newton's job was bad and John was bad too. He said bad words and did bad things - and he did not want to be Jesus' friend ...

But then ... one day ... his boat was on the sea with bigger waves than he had ever seen. The boat was breaking up. The boat was sinking. John was scared. He asked Jesus to help him. The storm stopped! John said sorry for all the bad things he had done. Jesus forgave him! He became Jesus' friend.

John changed his job. He started telling other people about how they could be Jesus' friends too. He told people how cruel it was to sell people for money. He gave talks and wrote books. More and more people heard his amazing story. If he could be Jesus' friend anyone could be!

"The LORD sustains them on their sick-bed
and restores them from their bed of illness."

Psalm 41:3

Florence Nightingale
(1820-1910)

Have you ever been in a hospital? Were you visiting or were you a patient? Did you see nurses helping people?

When Florence Nightingale was a girl hospitals in England were nasty and dirty. The nurses were sometimes nasty and dirty too and often didn't help people at all.

Florence's family was rich. They thought Florence should live like other rich girls - go to smart parties, wear smart clothes and play with smart friends. But Florence was Jesus' friend. She knew that Jesus didn't want her to just live like that - he wanted her to help people. Florence wanted to be a nurse and help people who were ill. Florence's parents were very cross. Rich girls weren't supposed to be nurses in nasty, dirty hospitals. But Florence wanted to make hospitals clean and safe - somewhere people got better not worse.

Florence got her big chance when she went to look after ill and wounded soldiers in the Crimea in Russia. She made sure the hospitals were clean and safe, not nasty and dirty. She taught nurses how to make people better not worse. When she came home she set up a special school to teach more nurses how to care for people.

Today hospitals are clean and safe places, where nurses help and care, and where people usually get better not worse - thanks to Florence Nightingale who wanted to do something for her friend Jesus.

"The LORD works righteousness
and justice for all the oppressed."
Psalm 103:6

Do you sometimes think life is unfair? When someone has a bigger piece of cake than you, or has nicer toys?

Life was very unfair for Rosa Parks. She knew that her friend Jesus treated all people the same - but in Alabama in America, when she lived, people definitely weren't all treated the same. Rosa and her family couldn't live in nice places, go to nice schools or eat in nice restaurants - just because they were black. They couldn't swim in the same swimming pools as white people. They couldn't play in the same parks as white people. They couldn't even sit in the same part of a train or bus! Rosa knew this was not what her friend Jesus wanted.

One day she was asked to move from her seat on the bus so that a white person could sit there. She said, "No". She didn't shout or hit - Jesus wouldn't want that. She just said, "No". The police asked her to move. She was very polite - but she still said, "No". She went to prison for saying, "No"; for saying she would not move seats; for saying that black people should be treated the same as white people like Jesus wanted. Lots of other people now said "No" too. Little by little life became less unfair for black people in America - because Jesus' friend Rosa said, "No".

"The LORD is with me; I will not be afraid.
What can mere mortals do to me?"

Psalm 118:6

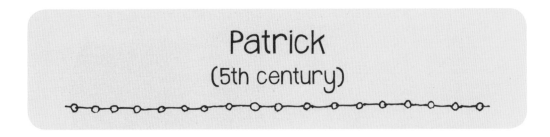

Patrick
(5th century)

Have you ever felt frightened and all alone? Perhaps you got lost and felt worried and afraid.

Patrick knew just what that felt like. Patrick lived a long time ago, when England was a very dangerous place. One day some pirates took him away from his family; they took him across the sea to Ireland, and sold him to a rich, fierce and powerful man. Patrick was frightened and all alone, but he knew that Jesus was with him. After many years Jesus helped Patrick go home to his family - but not for long! Patrick knew Jesus wanted the people in Ireland to find out how they could be his friends too.

So Patrick went back to Ireland. This time he wasn't scared. This time he was brave. This time he knew he had a job to do for Jesus. Patrick went to the richest, the fiercest and the most powerful men in Ireland. He went to the kings and chiefs. He told them about Jesus - the king of kings and chief of chiefs! The powerful people told the less powerful people that they should listen to Patrick too. Soon thousands and thousands of people had become Jesus' friends because Patrick was brave enough to tell them how.

Patrick knew he could be brave if Jesus was with him. Do you?

"Come, my children, listen to me;
I will teach you the fear of the LORD."
Psalm 34:11

Robert Raikes
(1736-1811)

What do you like doing at school? Reading? Writing? Numbers? Playtime?

In England, when Robert Raikes was alive, almost no children went to school at all. Poor children worked all day on Monday, Tuesday, Wednesday, Thursday, Friday and Saturday in factories to earn money for their families. Sunday was their only free day - and on Sunday lots of the children just caused trouble!

Robert Raikes wanted to help. Robert owned his town's newspaper - as he thought reading was important. He was Jesus' friend - he thought Jesus was even more important! He wanted poor children to learn to read and write, and to learn about his friend Jesus. So Robert set up a school on Sundays so they could learn - and to keep them out of trouble! In the morning they learnt reading and writing. In the afternoon they went to church and learnt about Jesus from the Bible.

He told people about the school in his newspaper. More and more children came. More and more schools were started. More and more children learnt to read and write and learnt about Jesus. Soon thousands, then millions of children were learning in Sunday schools.

The government stopped children working all week and said they could go to school from Monday to Friday instead - but lots of the children kept going to Sunday school to learn all about Jesus!

"One generation commends your works to another;
they tell of your mighty acts."
Psalm 145:4

Rembrandt
(1606-1669)

Do you like drawing and painting and colouring in? What do you like drawing best? Animals? Cars? People?

Rembrandt liked drawing and painting. He was brilliant at it. He became one of the best drawers and painters in the world ever! In his country, Holland, at that time most people drew pictures of flowers, pictures of towns and pictures of the countryside. What Rembrandt liked drawing and painting best were stories from the Bible - and pictures of himself!

He drew pictures of all the famous stories in the Bible. He drew Old Testament stories - Adam and Eve; Abraham; Joseph; Moses; Jonah; Esther; Ruth; Daniel; and more! He drew New Testament stories - the Good Samaritan; the Prodigal Son; Mary and Martha. Most of all he liked drawing pictures of his friend Jesus - Jesus teaching; Jesus making people better; Jesus with little children; Jesus on the cross - and lots of pictures just of Jesus' head!

Like us Rembrandt didn't live when Jesus was alive on earth, so he didn't know what Jesus looked like, but he wanted to show what he might have looked like. Rembrandt showed that Jesus is a real person - someone who can understand how we are feeling, and someone we can know and talk to.

Why don't you see if you can draw a picture of your favourite Bible story?

"The law from your mouth is more precious to
me than thousands of pieces of silver and gold."

Psalm 119:72

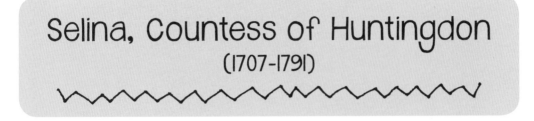

Selina, Countess of Huntingdon
(1707-1791)

If you had more money than you could ever dream of, what would you do with it? Would you buy toys, or games, or presents for your friends?

Selina, Countess of Huntingdon had more money than most people could ever dream of. She was very, very rich; her house was very, very big; her friends were very, very important. She was even friends with the king and queen! Then she became Jesus' friend. She knew that being Jesus' friend was far better than being very, very rich; better than having a very, very big house; better than having very, very important friends.

Selina wanted everyone to know how they could be Jesus' friends too. She wanted rich people to learn about Jesus; she wanted poor people to learn about Jesus. She wanted people in England to learn about Jesus; she wanted people in other countries to learn about Jesus. So she gave her money away.

She gave her money to build churches where all kinds of people could learn about Jesus. She gave her money to men who would teach people about Jesus in England. She gave her money to men who could teach people about Jesus in other countries. She had no more money - but because of Selina, Jesus had lots more friends!

"Defend the weak and the fatherless; uphold
the cause of the poor and the oppressed."

Psalm 82:3

Lord Shaftesbury
(1801-1885)

Do you have to do chores at home? What is the worst job? Tidying your room? Laying the table? Helping in the garden?

Two hundred years ago, in England, children did some horrible jobs - not just sometimes, but all day, every day! Some worked all day, every day down dark, dirty and dangerous mines. Some worked all day, every day up dark, dirty and dangerous chimneys. Some worked all day, every day in dusty, dingy and dangerous factories.

Lord Shaftesbury was an important man; he was from an important family; he was a Member of Parliament - and he was Jesus' friend. He knew his friend Jesus loved children - so Lord Shaftesbury used his important job to help them. He found out as much as he could about the children's jobs - how long they worked; how much they were paid; what work they did. He tried to change laws so children didn't have to work all day, every day in dark, dirty and dangerous places.

Bit by bit the laws were changed. Young children weren't allowed to work in mines; young children weren't allowed to work up chimneys; young children weren't allowed to work at all! Now children could learn instead of work - so there was a law that said all young children must go to school.

Lord Shaftesbury helped make children's lives safer, easier and more fun! Thank you, Lord Shaftesbury!

"Though my father and mother forsake me,
the LORD will receive me."

Psalm 27:10

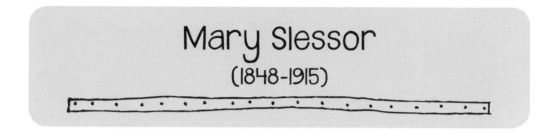

Mary Slessor
(1848-1915)

Do you know any twins? Any brothers and sisters the same age as each other? I am a twin. I have a twin brother. I think being a twin is quite special.

A hundred years ago in Nigeria in Africa, people didn't think twins were special at all. People hated twins and wanted to get rid of them when they were born - but God sent Mary Slessor to help these babies. Even though Mary was very poor, even though Mary was born in Scotland - a long, long way from Africa - and even though Mary was a young woman all on her own, God used her to help save hundreds and hundreds of twin babies.

Mary travelled to Africa. Mary travelled to places other people thought were too far away and too scary. She was a long, long way from home, she was poor and she was a young woman all on her own, but she wanted to tell the people there that her friend Jesus loved them too. She showed them that her friend Jesus loved twins as well. She took twins that nobody wanted and looked after them - caring for hundreds and hundreds of babies. She became famous in Nigeria for helping all kinds of people in all kinds of ways, but I think helping all those twin babies was the best!

"Then I will teach transgressors your ways,
so that sinners will turn back to you."

Psalm 51:13

Charles Spurgeon
(1834-1892)

Do you like talking and chatting and telling people things?

Charles Spurgeon was very good at talking, but not just about anything. Charles Spurgeon was very good at talking about his friend Jesus. Charles became Jesus' friend when he was fifteen. Just a few months later he gave his first talk about Jesus in church. Just a few months after that he was asked to lead the church! More and more people came to hear Charles - they loved to hear him talk about Jesus.

Soon Charles was asked to lead a big church in London. After just a few months the building was not big enough for everyone who wanted to hear Charles talk about Jesus, so they built a bigger one - for thousands of people! Newspapers printed Charles' talks so that people could read them too. In his talks Charles told people how to become Jesus' friends. In his talks Charles told Jesus' friends how they could love and trust him more. In his talks Charles helped people understand God's word the Bible. He set up a college to help more people teach the Bible like he did.

Some important people didn't like Charles - they said his talks were too exciting without any long words and too much of the Bible! But ordinary people loved him for telling them about Jesus.

"Not to us, LORD, not to us but to your name be
the glory, because of your love and faithfulness."
Psalm 115:1

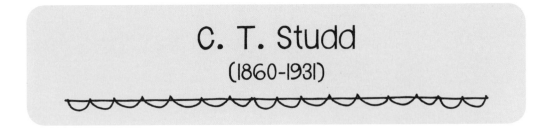

C. T. Studd
(1860-1931)

Do you have a favourite sport? Football? Tennis? Maybe cricket?

In England, a hundred and fifty years ago, cricket was the favourite sport. If you were good at cricket you were a hero - and C. T. Studd was the best cricketer in the whole country! C. T. was Jesus' friend, but he was so busy playing cricket and being rich and famous that he sometimes forgot he was Jesus' friend at all.

Then, one day, C. T.'s brother nearly died. C. T. realised that his brother would not last forever; cricket would not last forever; fame and fortune would not last forever; only his friend Jesus would last forever. So C. T. decided to live his life telling people about Jesus. He gave up cricket; he gave up fame; he even gave away all his money - and went to China to tell people about Jesus.

He was very ill and came home to England. His friends thought he would stay and rest, and be safe and comfortable - but C. T. wanted to keep telling people about Jesus. He went to India to tell people about Jesus there. He was very ill again and came home - maybe this time he would stay. But C. T. went to the very middle of Africa to tell people there about his friend Jesus. He knew that being Jesus' friend was better than fame, fortune and even cricket!

"All the ends of the earth will remember and turn to the LORD,
and all the families of the nations will bow down before him ..."
Psalm 22:27

Hudson Taylor
(1832-1905)

Do you like dressing up? What is your favourite costume - a princess, or a super hero, or a cowboy?

Hudson Taylor dressed up, but not just for fun. Hudson Taylor wore different clothes to help him tell people about his friend Jesus. Hudson knew that everyone in every country in the world needed to hear how they could be Jesus' friend. He wanted to tell people in China. China was a long, long way away. China had a different language, different food and different clothes.

Hudson went to China. Hudson learnt Chinese languages, ate Chinese food and wore Chinese clothes. Some of his friends thought this was a very strange thing to do - but Hudson knew it would help him tell the Chinese people all about Jesus. Hudson travelled all over China - it was very dangerous and very hard work.

He couldn't tell everyone in China about Jesus all on his own. So he asked if any of Jesus' friends in England would come and help him - even though it was dangerous; even though it was hard work; even though they would have to dress up in Chinese clothes. Some people said yes!

More and more people in China heard about Jesus because of Hudson Taylor. Sometimes dressing up is a really good idea!

"Let the morning bring me word of your unfailing love, for I have put my trust in you. Show me the way I should go, for to you I entrust my life."

Psalm 143:8

Lilias Trotter
(1853-1928)

If you could choose what to do today what would you choose? Playing outside or inside? Watching TV or reading a book? Sometimes it's hard to choose.

Lilias Trotter knew she had to choose what to do - not just for a day, but for her whole life. Lilias loved painting - she was very good at it, and painting is a good thing to do. Lilias also loved telling people about her friend Jesus, and that is a good thing to do too. Should she spend her life as a painter and become rich and famous, or should she spend her life telling people about Jesus and be poor and unknown? What would you choose? Lilias knew that painting was good, but telling people about Jesus was even better. That's what she chose to do.

Lilias went all the way to North Africa. The people there were Muslims who didn't know about Jesus - so she told them in every way she could think of! She started sewing clubs and coffee shops; she travelled to tiny villages and tents in the desert; she made friends with women and children; she wrote little books and decorated them with her beautiful pictures. She did all this to tell people about her friend Jesus - and some of those people became Jesus' friends too. Lilias certainly made the right choice!

"In God, whose word I praise - In God I trust and
am not afraid. What can mere mortals do to me?"

Psalm 56:4

William Tyndale
(1494-1536)

What is your favourite Bible story? Is it Noah's Ark or David and Goliath? The feeding of the five thousand or the healing of the blind man? I wonder what you would choose!

There was a time in England when children couldn't read Bible stories - and if someone read them out loud it was no use, because they were written in a very old language that only a few people could understand. How could people learn how to be Jesus' friends if they couldn't read what God said in the Bible?

William Tyndale was very clever and understood lots of old languages. He wanted to put the Bible into words that ordinary boys and girls and grown-ups could understand. The king told him he wasn't allowed to and got very angry! William had to run away to another country and pretend he was someone else, but he didn't give up his plan. The king's spies tried to stop him, but he didn't give up.

William worked and worked for months and months and months. At last it was finished! The new Bible was taken secretly back to England. Now people could finally read God's word in their own language - but the king's spies had caught up with William. He died for wanting ordinary people to be able to read about Jesus.

"He put a new song in my mouth, a hymn of praise to our God. Many will see and fear the LORD and put their trust in him."

Psalm 40:3

Charles Wesley
(1707-1788)

Do you like singing songs at Christmas? Which is your favourite? "Jingle Bells" is fun, but the songs about baby Jesus are better!

One of the most famous songs about baby Jesus was written by Charles Wesley. He wrote "Hark the Herald Angels Sing" nearly three hundred years ago, and millions of Jesus' friends still sing it every year to celebrate Jesus' birthday.

Charles, like his brother John Wesley, grew up thinking that if he was really good and went to church a lot Jesus might want to be his friend. When he found out that Jesus loved him so much already that he died on the cross for him, Charles was so happy. He was so happy that the very next day he wrote another of his famous songs, "And Can It Be", to show how brilliant it was to be Jesus' friend.

Charles, like John, travelled all over the place telling people about Jesus. But while he travelled Charles wrote songs too - Christmas songs, Easter songs, happy songs and sad songs. Every song was all about his friend Jesus. Every song helped people love and trust Jesus more. Every song helped people think about Jesus as they sang together at church, or on their own at home, at work, at school, or in the bath. No wonder we still sing his songs today!

"Surely his salvation is near those who fear him,
that his glory may dwell in our land."

Psalm 85:9

Does your church meet in a big building or a small building? Is it old or new? Are the seats comfy or hard?

When John Wesley was growing up he went to church in a big, beautiful, old building. He liked church; he liked doing churchy things; he was very well behaved - but he wasn't Jesus' friend. One day he found out from the Bible that he could be Jesus' friend - not because he liked church, churchy things and being good, but because Jesus died on the cross for him.

John wanted everyone to know how they could be Jesus' friends too. He told people in big, beautiful, old buildings - but often they didn't want to know and were very mean to him. They liked being churchy and well behaved, but weren't interested in being Jesus' friends at all - so John went into fields and barns, town squares and halls. He travelled thousands and thousands of miles, year after year after year - all over England, Ireland, Scotland and Wales. He told thousands and thousands of people all about Jesus, from morning to night. Some of these people didn't want to know and were very mean to him, but thousands and thousands listened and thousands and thousands became Jesus' friends.

We can meet in a beautiful building, a shabby hut or even outdoors - what matters is that we are Jesus' friends.

"I will perpetuate your memory through all generations;
therefore the nations will praise you for ever and ever."
Psalm 45:17

Susanna Wesley
(1669-1742)

How many children are there in your family? Are there lots or is there just you?

Susanna Wesley came from a very big family. She had twenty-four brothers and sisters! It must have been very noisy. Jesus was her best friend. However busy she was, however noisy it was, however much fun she was having, she always found time to talk to him and find out about him in the Bible.

When she was grown up she had nineteen children of her own! She had to work very hard - looking after the big children; looking after the little children; looking after the babies; cooking food; cleaning the house. She was very busy! Jesus was still her best friend. However busy she was, however noisy it was, however tired she was, she still always found time to talk to him and find out more about him in the Bible.

She knew that Jesus was the best friend ever. She wanted all her children to be his friends too. However busy she was, however noisy it was, however tired she was, she always found time to teach all her children all about Jesus - and how he could be their best friend too.

When they were grown up two of her children - John and Charles - spent their whole lives telling people about Jesus. She was a great mum!

"I do not hide your righteousness in my heart; I speak of your faithfulness and your saving help. I do not conceal your love and your faithfulness from the great assembly." Psalm 40:10

George Whitefield
(1714-1770)

Have you ever been in a very big crowd of people? What did you go to see? Perhaps a football match, or a fireworks display?

When George Whitefield was around thousands and thousands and thousands of people went to see him! He didn't look very special and he wasn't a king or a film star or a footballer, but he was very good at telling people about Jesus. As soon as George learnt how he could be Jesus' friend, he wanted everyone else to know too. Most people listened to him telling them how they could be Jesus' friends - but some of them threw smelly vegetables at him to make him stop.

George never stopped. He travelled on his horse all over England and Wales and Scotland. He travelled on a boat over the sea to America. Crowds and crowds of people came to hear him wherever he went. He talked about Jesus in churches; he talked about Jesus in fields. He talked about Jesus in the sunshine; he talked about Jesus in the pouring rain. He talked about Jesus when he was well; he talked about Jesus when he was ill. He talked about Jesus to rich people; he talked about Jesus to poor people - and lots of those people became Jesus' friends.

Hearing about Jesus is far better than football or fireworks!

"The LORD works righteousness
and justice for all the oppressed."
Psalm 103:6

William Wilberforce
(1759-1833)

Do you sometimes feel sad when you see bad things happening? Do you want to help when your friends are hurt, or upset, or sad?

When William Wilberforce was growing up he only thought about himself - how he could have fun; how he could become famous and important. He had lots of fun and he did become important. He became a Member of Parliament - someone who helps decide the country's laws.

Then ... he became Jesus' friend. Now he wanted to help other people, not just himself. What could he do? Who could he help? In those days people from Africa were taken prisoner, put on ships and taken far away to be sold - like things, not like people at all. William knew that this was very wrong. Maybe he could use his important job to change the country's laws - then selling people would have to stop.

William worked and worked and worked. He gave talks; he wrote letters; he wrote laws. People didn't listen. The laws didn't change. He gave more talks; he wrote more letters; he wrote more laws. He worked and worked and worked. He worked for years and years and years. At last people listened. At last the laws were changed. People could not be taken and sold anymore.

William wanted to help because he was Jesus' friend.
Who could you help today?

"May the groans of the prisoners come before you;
with your strong arm preserve those condemned to die."

Psalm 79:11

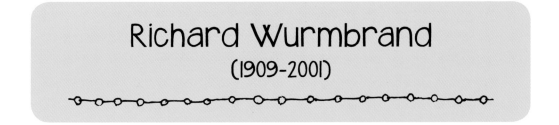

Richard Wurmbrand
(1909-2001)

Do you like being on your own or being with lots of people? Being on your own for an hour is OK, but what about for a day? A week? A year?

Richard Wurmbrand was all on his own for years and years. He was all alone, and not allowed to talk to a single person. He was all alone, not allowed to talk to a single person, and in prison. He was all alone, not allowed to talk to a single person, in prison, where people hurt him. Why? Because Richard wanted people in his country, Romania, to find out about his friend Jesus.

In Romania, in those days, the people in charge tried to stop anyone being Jesus' friend. When Richard said they were wrong, and told people about Jesus anyway, he was put in prison, all alone, for years and years. But in prison he was never really alone - his friend Jesus was always with him.

After years and years Richard was let out of prison, and let out of Romania. Richard then worked for years and years to help people in countries, like Romania, where it was hard to be Jesus' friend. He wrote and spoke and prayed and sent Bibles. He reminded them that with Jesus as your friend, you are never really on your own.

"The law of the LORD is perfect, refreshing the soul.
The statutes of the LORD are trustworthy, making wise the simple."

Psalm 19:7

John Wycliffe
(About 1334-1384)

Have you ever been told you couldn't do something because you weren't old enough? To play a game? Join a club? Go on a scary ride?

When John Wycliffe was alive most people in England weren't allowed to read the Bible - not because they weren't old enough, but because they weren't church leaders. The church leaders should have helped the people find out about Jesus - how he loved them; how he died for them; how they could be his friends - but they didn't! They should have shown the people how to follow Jesus by being kind and humble and gentle - but they didn't!

John Wycliffe was a church leader - but he was different. He read the Bible and saw that other church leaders had got things wrong. He read the Bible and saw that church leaders should be kind and humble and gentle, not rich and proud and mean. He read the Bible and saw that ordinary people could be Jesus' friends by trusting in him, not by just doing whatever church leaders told them. John wanted ordinary people to read the Bible so they could find this out for themselves. Until then the Bible had only been written in the old language of Latin. His friends wrote out the Bible in English - the language of the ordinary people.

The church leaders hated John, but the ordinary people loved him for helping them know Jesus through the Bible.

"But with you there is forgiveness,
so that we can, with reverence, serve you."

Psalm 130:4

Do you worry about things? If you do, what do you worry about? School? Friends? Other stuff?!

Katharina Zell was a worrier. Katharina wanted to be Jesus' friend. Church leaders said she had to try really hard and maybe, just maybe, she would be good enough for Jesus. Katharina worried and worried and tried and tried - but she could never be sure she was quite good enough.

Then the Bible arrived in Strasbourg - the town where she lived - written in Katharina's own language. Finally she could find out how to be Jesus' friend for herself. She found out that Jesus died so that she could be his friend - she didn't have to try and try and worry and worry at all.

Now, because Katharina knew she was Jesus' friend, she wanted to try and try to be more like him. She helped her husband, Matthias, look after the people of Strasbourg. She looked after people who were ill; she wrote to people who were worried; she fed people who were hungry; she gave a home to people with nowhere to live; she helped other women understand the Bible so they could find out how to be Jesus' friends too.

Katharina still worried sometimes, but she knew that she was Jesus' friend - and that was what mattered most of all.

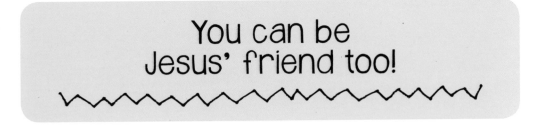

You can be Jesus' friend too!

Can you remember when you were really little - when you couldn't even walk or talk? Grown-ups had to help you with everything. Without their help you wouldn't have been able to do the things you wanted to do.

Jesus said that everyone who wants to be his friend needs to be like a child - even grown-ups! That doesn't mean everyone has to be a particular size or age - but it does mean everyone has to see that they need Jesus to help them.

When Jesus was on earth he did things only God can do - he stopped storms with just a whisper, he helped people who no doctors could help, he even made dead people alive again! No one else could do that - only Jesus. When no one else could help, Jesus could. Wouldn't you like a friend like that? If we want to be Jesus' friends we need to ask him to help us with our sin. Sin is a little word, but it is a big problem. It's when we think we know better than Jesus and want to do things our way not his. We can't be Jesus' friends if we are like that, because Jesus never did anything wrong! But Jesus wants us to be his friends so much that he died on the cross to forgive our sin so we can be his friends forever. We need to be sorry for our sin and ask Jesus to forgive us, asking him to help us do things his way not ours.

All the people in this book were Jesus' friends. They weren't perfect, but with God's help they tried to do things Jesus' way. Have you asked Jesus to forgive you and be your friend? I wonder what things you might do for your friend Jesus?

"Truly I tell you, anyone who will not receive the kingdom of God like a little child will never enter it."

Mark 10:15

TRUTH FOR LIFE®

THE BIBLE-TEACHING MINISTRY OF **ALISTAIR BEGG**

The mission of Truth For Life is to teach the Bible with clarity and relevance so that unbelievers will be converted, believers will be established, and local churches will be strengthened.

Daily Program

Each day, Truth For Life distributes the Bible teaching of Alistair Begg across the U.S., and in several locations outside of the U.S. on over 1,600 radio outlets. To find a radio station near you, visit **truthforlife.org/station-finder**.

Free Teaching

The daily program, and Truth For Life's entire teaching archive of over 2,000 Bible-teaching messages, can be accessed for free online and through Truth For Life's full-feature mobile app. A daily app is also available that provides direct access to the daily message and daily devotional. Download the free mobile apps at **truthforlife. org/app** and listen free online at **truthforlife.org**.

At-Cost Resources

Books and full-length teaching from Alistair Begg on CD, DVD and MP3CD are available for purchase at cost, with no mark up. Visit **truthforlife.org/store**.

Where To Begin?

If you're new to Truth For Life and would like to know where to begin listening and learning, find starting point suggestions at **truthforlife.org/firststep**. For a full list of ways to connect with Truth For Life, visit **truthforlife.org/subscribe**.

Contact Truth For Life

P.O. Box 398000 Cleveland, Ohio 44139
phone 1 (888) 588-7884   **email** letters@truthforlife.org
 /truthforlife   @truthforlife   **truthforlife.org**

Also in this series:

Everything a Child Should Know About God

Everything a Child Should Know About Prayer
(forthcoming)

10 Publishing

a division of 10ofthose.com

10Publishing is the publishing house of 10ofThose.
It is committed to producing quality Christian
resources that are biblical and accessible.

www.10ofthose.com is our online retail arm selling
thousands of quality books at discounted prices.

For information contact: sales@10ofthose.com

or check out our website: www.10ofthose.com